Photo Plots
How to write great
photo-inspired books and stories

by Gloria G. Adams

Photo Plots
How to write great
photo-inspired books and stories

ISBN-13: 978-1-7324659-9-2

Disclaimer: writing books or stories following
the Photo Plots Method does not guarantee
that persons will become published by a publishing house
or represented by a literary agent.

Copyright © 2018
by Gloria G. Adams
Images: Pixabay.com
All rights reserved. This book or any portion thereof may not
be reproduced or used in any manner whatsoever
without the express written permission of the publisher.

Slanted Ink

Stow, OH 44224

www.slantedink.com

To Jean, Joan and LeeAnn

CONTENTS

Introduction   1

CHAPTER ONE: THE BASICS   2

CHAPTER TWO: THE METHOD   11

CHAPTER THREE: A SAMPLE STORY   16

CHAPTER FOUR: ONE PHOTO, THREE STORIES   24

CHAPTER FIVE: THE PHOTOS: SETTINGS   36

CHAPTER SIX: THE PHOTOS: CHARACTERS   52

CHAPTER SEVEN: RESOURCES FOR WRITERS   70

INTRODUCTION

PHOTO PLOT: A story plot inspired by a photo.

PHOTO PLOTTING: The act of creating a story plot inspired by a photo.

PHOTO PLOTTER: One who photo plots.

There are times in the writing life when ideas dry up, when inspiration won't come. Your brain has come up with what you consider to be a fabulous idea, but no words seem to convey the vision you have for it. Maybe you're part way through your manuscript and nothing is working right in chapter eight. Or seven. Your mind is blank and so is that white page in front of you. Some call it "writer's block." No matter what you call it, it can be a source of great frustration.

One way to push through writer's block is to just start writing. And sometimes you need a prompt to get you going. I'm a big fan of word prompts, but sometimes they just aren't enough.

I find that photos work much better, possibly because they tap into the emotions through a visual experience. You can actually see the character, envision the scenery, smell the scent of those flowers. From there, hopefully, a story idea will germinate.

But, let's take it one step further. The picture is there, the ideas begin to flow, but where do you start and how do you actually make it work?
Try Photo Plots.

With Photo Plots, you can choose a picture, brainstorm some ideas, then fill in a special plot template, answering questions about characters, plot, and world building as you go.

You'll get some basics, step-by-step guides, a sample story built with the template, and three stories written by three different authors using the same photograph. Plus many wonderful photos to inspire you.

Whatever your experience with photo prompts has been, Photo Plots will take you a step further by providing the tools you need to build the stories only you can create. Ready? Let's get Photo Plotting!

CHAPTER ONE: THE BASICS

Begin with the basics: plot, character development, and setting/world building.

PLOT is the skeleton of your story, the bones around which everything else is built and the structure that holds everything together. There are many different plot structures you can follow, but whichever you choose, they all have similar basic elements. For the purposes of this book, we will look at plots for fiction books and stories.

Plots begin with the status quo. What defines the world in which your characters live? What do they do every day, and who/what else is part of their world?

Once the status quo is established, something has to happen to shake up that world and those characters, to cause them problems, to place obstacles in the way of what they want. That's the author's job: to create conflict and mayhem, to change the character's world forever, forcing him or her to take some sort of action. This is commonly called the "inciting incident."

The scenes that follow should take the character on his or her journey, the plan of action, to reach the goal, solve the problem, overcome the adversity, whatever you've given the characters to do. If you want to keep your reader's interest, you will move your narrative along with increasing tension, sometimes adding to your characters' problems, with obstacles and/or adversaries, until they reach that place they've been working toward: the climax. Following that is the resolution of the problem and the wrap up and ending. Often, there is an unexpected twist that, hopefully, the reader never saw coming.

There are several plot structures from which you may want to choose. The most basic plot is the three-act plot, with beginning, middle, and end. But except in the simplest of stories, you will need a more detailed plot. Most plots follow something similar to the following seven points. This is the plot structure on which the Photo Plots Method is based.

1. Hook, a sentence or two, the purpose of which is to grab the reader's attention and "hook" him or her into the story.
2. Set-up, or what life is like every day for the main character (s).
3. Inciting incident, an event that changes everything.
4. Rising action, several steps that the characters take on their journey to right or resolve whatever problem the inciting incident has caused. Each step should increase the tension.
5. Climax, which is the turning point of the story.
6. Falling action, in which the tension decreases and the characters move toward restoring order or bringing their world back to a "new normal."
7. Resolution/wrap-up/ending.

Hook

The hook is sometimes the first thing you think of to begin your story. Often, though, the hook is written last, after you have finished your story, and realize you might need to begin a different way or at a different place.

Hooking a reader in can be a challenge; below are a few ways to grab your reader's attention right from the beginning.

- Begin with the action. Throw your reader right into one of the most tense scenes from your book.

- Use a phrase that tells the reader that something is different or unusual about this world. This works especially well with science fiction and fantasy. For example, "The wolf spoke to the woman quietly, softly, weaving a spell with words that drew her to him like a moth to a flame."

- Give clues to a secret that the reader will want to find out.

- Begin with a question. "Exactly how many people *have* you killed, Henry?"

- Start in the midst of a natural disaster, such as a hurricane or fire.

- Keep it simple and, generally, use active voice. Short statements, big punch.

- Make it appropriate for your target audience.

- Check out other books to find effective hooks. For example, in *Paradise*, by Toni Morrison, the first line reads, "They shoot the white girl first."

Setup

The purpose of the setup is to let your reader know about the world you've created, as well as the characters. There are several things to keep in mind regarding your setup.

- Use the setup to create interest in your setting and characters.
- Don't give all the information all at once at the beginning of the book or story. Spread details throughout the first few chapters and even further along.
- Use dialogue as well as narrative to inform your reader.
- Give enough information to make your reader understand and care about what is going to happen to your characters.

Setup can be complex for science fiction and fantasy worlds and characters. The best authors create believable worlds without overwhelming the reader. The important word to remember with setup is **balance.** Stretch out what you teach us about the world of your story, and don't tell us everything all at once.

Inciting Incident

Nothing is ever the same for your character or characters after the inciting incident. Their world has changed and it will never go back to what it used to be. It creates the conflict that is the basis for everything that follows; it's what motivates the main character to take the actions that move the story along.

Think about the inciting incidents from famous stories: the tornado swirling onto Dorothy's farm in The Wizard of Oz, Mark Watney being injured and left behind on Mars in The Martian, Nick Dunne finding that his wife is missing in Gone Girl.

The inciting incident can be something that happens to your main character or it could be an act by your main character that results in some sort of consequence. Whatever it is that happens, it changes that character's world forever and sets the action in motion.

At this point, you will want to determine the goals/desires of your main character in regards to the inciting incident.

Rising Action

Rising action is the meat of your story. Each action taken by the main character should move the story forward. It should also increase the tension of your story. Think of it as stair steps that will lead to the final resolution of the problem, or the destination reached, or the goal realized.

For example, in The Lord of the Rings trilogy, Frodo's goal is to reach Mount Doom and throw the Ring into the fire. Along the way, he has to fight many battles and overcome many obstacles to reach his destination. It gets harder and harder and we wonder if he will ever make it there. The tension lasts right to the last minute.

Raising the stakes makes for good rising action. If everything comes too easily for your main character, or someone else solves things for him or her, there's not enough conflict to make the story interesting or keep your reader engaged. When things are going too well, throw another obstacle in your character's path. Give him or her hard choices with something to lose and difficult consequences.

Climax

The climax of a story is what your reader has been waiting for. Will the two characters finally fall in love with each other? Will the action hero survive and win the battle? Will the detective solve the mystery? Will the prince ever find the woman who lost the glass slipper?

There are several things to remember about the climax.

- Place the climax near the end of the book.
- Don't cheat the reader. If you have dropped clues throughout the

book as to who killed the murder victim, don't have it turn out to have simply been an accident. The reader wants to help solve the mystery by following the clues you gave him.

- Release the tension. The climax should be the moment you release the tension you built up during the rising action. This should be that "Ah-ha!" moment the reader has been waiting for.

Falling Action

The falling action is what occurs right after the climax. It is usually a short part of the book, but it can serve to answer questions about the effects on the characters of what happened in the climax, the aftermath of realizing their goal or reaching their destination. It gives your readers some closure and leads them to the resolution and ending. It also serves to keep the book from ending too abruptly.

For example, in the Wizard of Oz, the story doesn't end when Dorothy finally defeats the wicked witch and reaches the Emerald City. What follows is the falling action, with the three friends realizing their dreams of having a brain, a heart, and bravery, followed by Glenda telling Dorothy how to get back to Kansas.

Resolution/Wrap up/Ending

Finally, the resolution ties together all the loose ends and, hopefully, provides a satisfying ending of your main character's story. It can sometimes end in a set-up for a sequel or even in a surprising twist. However you decide to end your story, make sure it's one that will make your reader want to read your next book.

No matter how you decide to create your plot from the photo or photos you choose, the important thing to remember is that your plot is all about your reader. What do you want your reader to get out of your book? What do you want to say? How can you draw your reader into the world of the photo and make him or her care about your characters?

CHARACTERS can make or break a good story, so it's good to examine the elements that go into creating great characters.

One of the main things to remember about building characters for a fiction story or novel is that it's about **connection.** Your readers must feel a connection to your characters, enough to care about what happens to them. Otherwise, they won't stay with you and they won't finish reading your work.

Think about the characters that you remember from literature. What made them so memorable? What did you like/hate about them? Why did you care if they failed or succeeded? You need to look at *your* characters the same way.

Main characters are often brave or are trying to be brave. They may have great odds to overcome and it almost always involves having something to lose. In The Hunger Games, Katniss makes the decision to volunteer for the games in her sister's place in order to save Primrose. She knows she will probably die. She ends up as a leader who overthrows the evil government that is controlling the people through starvation and fear. She fights for the greater good, but also to save Prim. We want her to succeed because her motives are pure, but they are also very personal.

Your characters should not be perfect. If they are perfect, they will always do the right thing. No one can relate to that. While we may want to always do the right thing, our flaws usually come along and cause us to make mistakes, to be embarrassed or humiliated. Your characters suffer and all of us who are imperfect understand those feelings and suffer along with them. Your job as the author is to throw obstacles in the path so that your characters have to make hard decisions that will change them somehow.

Along with that, however, your characters and your reader want to experience success, triumph at overcoming those obstacles, a sense of accomplishment. We read, quite often, to live other people's lives.

Give your characters secrets and relate them to the main theme in your story. Secrets raise curiosity and entice the reader to find out what they are.

If you begin with a photo that has people in it, you will already have a lot of your physical characteristics taken care of. On the other hand, if you begin with just a setting, you will need to create all of the characters in that world. Once you describe those characteristics, you need to move on to what they are really like.

Treat them as though you know them. Talk to them and talk as though you were them. Put yourself in their shoes. How would they talk? What would they say? How would they react to different situations? How does it feel when they fail? When they succeed?

Make a list of characteristics you want for your characters. Are they generally happy, like Winnie-the-Pooh, or morose, like Eeyore? Do they live life to the fullest or do their fears and insecurities keep them from doing what they really want to do? Are they kind, compassionate, aloof, aggressive, outspoken, shy?

Once you've decided what your characters are like at the beginning of your story, write down what you want them to be like at the end. It will help you craft the rest of your story. It's like reading a map; once you know where you're going, it's easier to figure out how to get there.

Whatever kinds of characters you create, keep your goal of connecting with your reader in the forefront.

- Give your characters motivations and goals that you would admire; give your antagonist evil motives that must be overcome.
- Give your characters something to lose, and character flaws that might jeopardize realizing their goals. What scares them? What motivates them? What makes them really uncomfortable?
- Take them through some experiences that are common to most people, as well as those that aren't.
- Throw obstacles in their path and make their struggles and motivations very personal.
- Sprinkle in a secret or even two that your characters are keeping.
- Fill up on sensory details to which everyone can relate.

Follow these suggestions and you've got a good formula for connecting with your reader.

SETTING/WORLD BUILDING is the third piece of the basics puzzle. The setting photos in this book range from historical to present day, with illustrations for fantasy and sci-fi. Whichever you pick, there are certain elements that the world of your characters must have.

One of the most important ones is **consistency**, especially when you create fantasy worlds that don't exist. But even with a setting that's familiar to you, there's a danger of changing details that you shouldn't. For example, if it's springtime in upper state New York, don't have your protagonist picking tomatoes or zucchini which aren't harvested until later in the summer. For fantasy or sci-fi, even though you can invent all sorts of strange people, creatures, and landscapes, make sure what you invent stays consistent throughout the book. If one of your magical creatures is blind, and can only discern what's around it by smell, make sure it isn't *looking* at something at another place in your book.

Setting can determine the mood of the book. Dark forests, damp caves, misty moors, and haunted castles have a completely different feel than bright, sunny meadows or a school playground with laughing children. Use your setting to bring out whatever feelings you want your reader to imagine.

The type of setting you choose can also supply one or more of the obstacles that your main character must overcome. Forest fires, tornadoes, hurricanes, volcanic eruptions, mud slides, floods, and avalanches are just some examples of ways your setting can serve as the reason your characters must conquer their fears and find their way out of a life-threatening situation. Or, it could be as simple as a mountain that must be climbed or a river that must be crossed.

Add sensory details to make your setting feel more real. Imagine yourself standing inside the picture you have chosen. What do you think your characters might smell, taste, see, or hear? What tactile details can you add? Does the moss on the tree move? Is it soft, as expected, or will it grab your hand and scratch you when you touch it? How cold is the snow? Does it blind you when the sun shines on it or does the shimmer of the sun on the snow crystals fill you with a feeling of euphoria? Whichever photo or illustration you choose, begin by jotting down the sensory details.

When considering each photo, look at the following elements as you build your world:

- Weather
- Geology
- Vegetation
- Animals
- Insects
- Birds
- Home structures
- Transportation
- Ethics
- Religion
- Money/trade
- Social structure
- Government

- Mythology/how this world came to exist
- Magic or magical creatures
- Food and clothing
- Time
- Language
- Technology

One of the biggest things to remember about telling the backstory or describing the setting is not to do it all at once at the beginning of your novel or story. Has that been done before? Yes, but it's an easy way to lose the reader unless it is so compelling that it holds the reader's interest unwaveringly. It's usually better to sprinkle information about your setting throughout your story, using other devices besides narrative, such as dialogue, actions or messages, to tell us about the world in which your book takes place.

CHAPTER 2: THE PHOTO PLOTS METHOD

How to Create a Story or Book from a Photo

Choose a photo (or illustration) and brainstorm the initial story ideas you get from the photo. Decide if you will write a short story or a novel. Will it be a children's story, teen story, or adult novel? Know how many words you will need to write:

- Picture books - approximately 500 to 1,000 words

- Easy/early readers - approximately 500 to 2,000 words

- Chapter books - approximately 3,000 to 10,000 words

- Middle grade novels - approximately 20,000 to 55,000 words

- Young adult novels - approximately 55,000 to 80,000 words

- Short stories – varies, 1,500 to 10,000 words

- Adult and New Adult – 75,000 to 90,000 words

Before you write the actual story, you will want to begin by doing three things:

1. Create your characters.

2. Describe your setting or world.

3. Build your plot.

1. Create your characters:

- If you are using a photo with people, describe the characters you see: eye color, hair color, size, gender, race, clothing.
- What does your character do for a living? Hobbies? If a child, does he or she go to school? Homeschooled? Is he or she homeless?
- Does this person have a religion? What is his or her world view?
- Write down what your character or characters like, what they hate, what scares them, what makes them happy, etc.
- Decide if they are shy, quiet, weak, bold, loud, strong, mean, kind, sensitive, narcissistic, etc.
- From whose point of view will you tell the story? Decide if you will use first person or third person.
- What are the relationships of the characters to one another?
- Ask yourself what you want your main character to be like by the end of the story, after experiencing whatever trouble you bring his/her way. Ask if your character has undergone an emotional change or come to a greater understanding of who he/she is. This is the emotional arc of your main character.
- Have you created characters to which your readers can relate? How will you make your readers care enough about what your characters want to stick with them to the end of the story or book?

2. Describe your setting or world

- Write down the details of the setting from the picture. What is the season? Time of day? Weather?
- If there is a town, what is it like? Big, small, urban, rural? What are the neighbors like, if there are any?
- How might the setting affect the story? For example, if it's winter, a blizzard could cause an accident or a hurricane could force people to stay together at a shelter where they might have conflicts.

- What are some elements of the mood of the story? What emotions does it convey?
- What sensory details can you draw from your setting to make it feel real to the reader?
- What kinds of characters might be part of this setting?

For settings/world building in science fiction/fantasy:

- Write down all the unusual details about the world that you see in the picture, as well as others that you create. Make sure you keep them consistent throughout the book/story.
- Are there animals or fantastical creatures in the picture? How do they relate to the characters and the physical world?
- How do people buy/trade in this world? What is important? How do they move around? What are the politics like? What behaviors are considered right and wrong? Is there a religion?

3. Build your plot:

- Open with a hook. What kind of statements will draw a reader into your book and make him/her want to keep reading?
- Design your setup. Where is your story set? Who is the main character? Who are your other characters?
- Inject an event that changes everything (the inciting incident.) What problem does this cause for your main character?
- Write down your main character's goal(s): what does he or she want or need to meet the goal/overcome the obstacle/ solve the problem? What steps does he/she believe will achieve this goal?
- Who(or what) stands in your main character's way? Why does he, she, or it want to keep your main character from achieving his or her goal?
- What are the main events that lead to the climax, the part where the main character achieves his or her goal, or perhaps even realizes that this goal is not what he or she really wanted?
- What choice/choices will your main character have to make that will result in what happens in the story as well as to your character's emotional growth?
- Resolve the end of the story. Is there a theme to your story? Good vs evil? Man vs nature? What do you want the reader to get from your story?

Story-building Template

Hook:
Setup/Everyday situation:
Inciting Incident:
Goal of main character: solve a problem/overcome an obstacle/reach a destination:
Rising Action/main events and character's choices:
Climax:
Falling action and resolution:

After you have filled in the template with the basics, you'll have the outline from which you can build your story. Go over the basics from Chapter One and answer as many of the questions in this chapter as you can.

The following two chapters offer examples of stories crafted from photos or illustrations using the Photo Plots Method.

CHAPTER THREE: A SAMPLE STORY

Using the picture below and the Story-building Template, I wrote a short story called Dragon's Lair. This could also be the basis for a two-book or even a three-book series.

Story-building Template

Hook: I smelled them before I saw them. The stench was so overpowering, I almost lost heart.

Setup/Everyday situation: A scouting group is deployed on a routine mission to spy on the status of a group of dragons in their lair.

Inciting Incident: The group discovers that all the females have borne whelps, which mature in a month, and, if they aren't killed now, will potentially destroy the castle and everyone in and around it.

Goal of main character: solve a problem/overcome an obstacle/reach a destination: The leader, Lila, plans to have their military forces attack and destroy all the dragons in the lair before they can attack the castle.

Rising Action: main events and character's choices: Lila chooses Felicia to send as a scout, which causes increasing tension between Lila and her daughter, Marion. During the night, Marion sneaks away to alert the strike force and possibly fight and maybe die with them. Lila must choose between defending the castle or going after and saving her daughter.

Climax: The castle is attacked, and Lila leads her soldiers back, but finds that the battle has just ended and they were successful in defeating the Greens. However, neither the strike force nor Marion has returned.

Falling Action and **Resolution**: Lila **waits** and watches through the whole day for Marion's return. Finally, in the evening, the scouts and part of the strike force return, victorious, along with Marion. Twist at the end.

Dragon's Lair
by Gloria G. Adams

I smelled them before I saw them. The stench was so overpowering, I almost lost heart. I glanced back at the others who were following me, searching for Marion. As if on cue, she raised her head and locked eyes with mine. Then she nodded. It was enough to give me the courage to move forward.

Marion was my firstborn, so close to my heart, and the one that was the most like me. At 15, she had joined me to serve together with eight others on the primary scouting party for Queen Isla's army. We had served her well so far and I counted myself fortunate to lead such a loyal and competent group of soldiers. We were the Sta-har, the all-female counterpart to the male scouts. Our advantage was that we were smaller and could maneuver the forest more easily.

And the forest was where we were now. I could barely make out the place where the trees gave rise to the hillock beyond which I knew we would find the Green Dragons' lair. Dusk was settling in and, in order to keep our cover, we planned to reach the hilltop before moonrise. As we neared the edge of the forest, I raised my arm to bring us to a halt. I scoured the slopes around the lair for guards, but didn't see any. It was one reason we always came this way; the Greens tended to watch the other side more diligently. Still, better to be cautious.

The stench was even stronger now. I was doubly thankful for the sap of the pink scallop tree with which the queen had insisted we cover our bodies. It masked our own scent and would effectively keep us hidden from the keen sense of smell of our adversary.

We spread out, as planned, and began crawling on our bellies, heads down, until we all reached the top of the hill. I was the first to peer over the edge and had to stifle a gasp at what I saw.

There were at least six times as many dragons as there had been the last time they had attacked us. I counted six males and twice as many females. But the most disturbing discovery was that all of the females had given birth since our last scouting mission. Surrounding each of the females were at least eight whelps. Most of them were male; I could tell by the bright orange triangle of scales that formed a protective covering over their throats.

I jumped at the loud whisper of Marion's voice next to me. "I count over a hundred all together. And at the rate the babes grow, they'll be ready to attack the castle in less than a month."

"I didn't hear you sneak up, Marion."

"Noted. You aren't losing your edge, are you, Mother? The queen might replace you as leader if you aren't more careful."

"Good thing you have my back, then."

"Always. But, look." She pointed skyward at the moon, which had come out while I was gawking at the spectacle below me. I signaled to the others and we melted back into the forest.

As we formed our usual circle, I stared hard at each scout before I spoke. "Our mission is clear. No choice. We'll have to call in a strike. I need a volunteer to alert the strike force. They need to attack tonight.."

Marion leapt forward. "I'll go, Mother!"

I was shocked at the wave of pain that washed over me. "Absolutely not! Your training's not quite finished."

"It's as good as done and you know it!" she shot back.

"Marion, do not contradict me. That's an order." I matched her fiery stare until, with a huff, she spun around and stomped off.

Daneera touched my arm. "No doubt you'll pay dearly for that decision, My Lady."

"No doubt."

Daneera grinned. "She's a lot like you were at that age."

"Don't remind me." I turned to the small band of scouts. "Who will go to alert the strike force? I won't order any of you. There's a good chance they'll want you to fight beside them, too."

"I'll go, My Lady." Felicia stepped forward. I wasn't surprised. She was the bravest and strongest scout I'd ever trained, but it would be hard to let her go. She was barely two years older than Marion.

I grasped both her arms and she, mine. "The queen's blessing on you, then, Child."

"The queen's blessing," murmured the others.

We touched foreheads and she gave my arm a squeeze as she turned away.

I watched until her small form disappeared from view, then turned to Daneera. "I need you to return to the castle and warn Queen Isla. Any males that escape the strike will surely attack the castle."

"As you wish. And, don't worry, Marion will come around. Queen's blessing, My Lady."

"Queen's blessing."

As Daneera set off toward the castle, the others headed back to our rally point. I hung back, searching for Marion. I found her, perched on a rock near a small stream, angrily flinging small stones into the water.

I sat down a few feet away. "I'm thinking this may not be the best way to show me how mature you are."

She didn't look at me. "You embarrassed me in front of the team."

"I know. And I'm sorry. You took me by surprise…"

"Oh, really, Mother! You knew it was just a matter of time before I went off on my own as a scout. It's what I've been training for, for Queen's sake! This is my time. You probably won't let me go next time, either!"

I tried to keep my voice light, but failed. "If we don't destroy most of the dragons in that lair right away, there may not be a next time, Marion. Now, come on, we need to get back to the others and set up a watch schedule."

She slammed a last handful of stones against the rock and stood up. "Fine."

I stayed where I was as she hurried into the woods, giving her time to get a long way ahead of me before I even stood up. By the time I reached the rally point, everyone except Shanali was asleep. "I can take first watch, My Lady."

"No, I'll do it, Shanali. Get some rest."

The silence and pine scent of the forest calmed me and I was more than ready to give up the watch when Shanali took over. A short while later, the terrified screams of the green dragons wrenched me out of a deep sleep. The first light of dawn revealed clouds of smoke rising above the trees from the lair and I searched the skies for any signs of escaping Greens. When I didn't see any, I turned to the others. "We're clear for now. Let's head back to the castle, in case some flew another way." I looked around. "Where's Marion?"

Shanali cleared her throat. "She's gone, My Lady. She must have snuck out while you slept. I'm so sorry. I never saw her go."

I closed my eyes, trying to keep the others from seeing the panic I was feeling. I knew she'd gone after Felicia, gone to join the strike force, gone to who knew what kind of fate. It took everything I had not to flee into the woods to find her and bring her back.

"Some of us are willing to go after her, My Lady, if you give the word." Shanali's eyes were full of tears. She knew how I felt. She had five children of her own.

For the first time in my life, I didn't know what to do. I'd always been the strong one, always so sure of myself and my decisions. Right now, all I wanted was to have Marion safely at my side again.

I took a deep breath. "Thank you, all of you. But…"

Suddenly, a loud screech splintered the air as a wall of flame shot through the trees not twenty feet away from us. I looked up just in time to see the spiked tail of a green dragon, soaring above the trees, headed for…

"The castle! Leave your gear! Let's go! NOW!"

The others followed me without a word, all of our military training kicking in. We raced toward the castle as fast as we could. As we got closer, we could see flame and smoke and hear cries and screams. Then suddenly, just before we reached the forest's edge, everything went silent.

The sight that greeted us as we burst into the clearing where the castle stood was not a pretty one. The castle walls were still shrouded in early morning mist, but not enough to hide the damage, nor the stench, caused by the marauding Greens.

I counted three of them, all dead. One floated in the moat, and two others lay broken and lifeless atop the crumpled remains of the south wall, their blood still dripping onto the ground below.

The battle had been fought and won before we'd even arrived. Even so, our comrades were still standing guard along the entire circumference of the castle. They greeted us as we crossed the drawbridge. Stellahar and Reach pushed open the great castle doors for me, and I hurried through them to find my queen.

Isla greeted me joyfully. "Lila! Thank the skies! You missed all the action, but because you sent Daneera back, we were ready. And you'll be glad to know we suffered no casualties."

"And the Greens? Did we destroy them all?"

"Still waiting on the report, but only three attacked us. Had the strike force failed, more would have come. Good job, my friend. We would never have survived had all the whelps reached full growth."

"And where is Daneera? Is she all right?"

"Good enough," said a voice from the hallway. Daneera limped into the room, leaning on a cane, half of one leg wrapped in bandages. "Where's Marion?"

I collapsed onto a bench, stifling a sob. "Gone. She left us in the night. To join the strike force, no doubt. And I didn't go after her! I…"

Daneera hobbled over to touch my shoulder. "You had to come back here, My Lady. To defend your queen."

"Yes." I raised my eyes to meet those of the queen. "What news have you of the strike force, Your Majesty?"

The queen's face fell. "None of the strike force has returned. I'm sorry, Lila."

"They may yet. I won't give up hope this soon." I rose and bowed to her, then went to go stand watch outside on the west balcony. This would be where they would return, if they returned at all. Daneera joined me, settling carefully on a bench behind me, and leaned her head against the stone wall.

The hours dragged on, my heart growing heavier with each one. Although Daneera slept most of the day, it was a comfort to have her there. The scout in me watched for the green shimmer of dragonscale in the sky, but none appeared.

Just as the sun began its daily descent, I saw movement through the trees.

Could it be? Yes! I recognized Dagger, leader of the strike force, and behind him, Ru-Ark, Jammison, and Felicia. Then, finally, to my great relief, Marion. She looked exhausted, dirty, but unhurt.

"Marion!"

She raised her head and grinned at me. When she mounted the steps, I could see the excitement in her eyes. "I did good, didn't I? We got them all, too! I know I worried you, but…"

Before she could finish, I grabbed her in a tight hug. "You did. And, you were right. I should have let you go. But, what about…I mean, besides not knowing if you'd been killed, I worried you'd be upset about slaughtering the whelps."

Marion pushed away and stared at me as though I'd lost my mind. "Are you kidding? Green Dragons are less than nothing. I mean, they'll never be as good as us. They're inferior in every way. Isn't that what you've always taught me, Mother?"

She laid one claw on the crimson scales of my arm. "I'm more proud to be a Red Dragon today than I've ever been!"

CHAPTER FOUR: ONE PHOTO, THREE STORIES

Three different authors were given the same photo and asked to write a short story using the photo as their inspiration and the Story-building Template as their guide. Below is the photo, followed by the stories.

COLD HOPE

by Margaret Maurer

The screen door to the garage slammed behind Luke as he stepped into the kitchen. Afternoon sunlight streamed sideways through the windows above the kitchen table, creating a cheery illusion of false warmth. He took his gloves off and rubbed his hands together. It was quiet. Too quiet. He wondered where Anna was.

Earlier the house had echoed with company, all gathered in town for their dad's funeral. His unexpected and instantly fatal heart attack had interrupted all their lives, and the remains from the week's chaotic events were scattered about the house. Dad's reading glasses still lay splayed open where he had left them near the television remote, as if they all expected him to come back and pick them up.

The silence was remarkably soothing now that they were done taking the last of the family to the airport.

But where was Anna? He called her name, checking from room to room. Not on the first floor, not in the basement. Out back? Perhaps, he thought. He zipped up his hoodie, grabbed his gloves, and headed out to the back yard, and the access path to the Metroparks behind their home. He thought he knew where she would go.

The ground was frozen cold, and a light dusting of snow crunched under his shoes. A path cut into the woods, bordered by waist-high undergrowth, young saplings and old-growth trees. Eventually it curved to the right, opening into a clearing where a large log faced a stone-cold firepit. And there was Anna.

Luke's sister was taller, and at 20, four years older. She sat on the log, facing away from him, head down, elbows on knees. Her blackish-brown hair shrouded her face. Her shoulders were hunched deeply into her down parka. In her hands was a bottle of beer, more than half gone. Luke frowned. He hesitated, but then knelt and hugged her from behind. Anna reached back to touch his arm. They stayed that way for a long time.

Anna was the first to speak. "Did you get them to the airport on time?"

"Yeah." Luke released her, rose and sat beside her on the log. His elbows braced on his knees, his hands clenched tight. Anna handed him the bottle and he drank, setting the beer bottle down between them on the ground.

"I'm glad we're alone. I'm glad he's gone," she said.

"Yeah."

"Luke, I'm sorry I left you here."

"You didn't have any choice."

"Yes, we did. No one else knew how much he drank. How he treated us, how he changed after mom died. I'm still shocked that no one knew. All those people here for the funeral, how they praised him. They'll never know. We could have told them. Or I could have stayed and gone to community college instead of taking the scholarship. But I didn't, we didn't. And you were left dealing with him."

"Maybe, but it was better that you left. He wasn't so angry after you left. I think you reminded him too much of mom, how much he missed her. Mostly he just went to work and drank." Luke picked up a stick from the ground and methodically began snapping it into small pieces. "I went to school and practice. He didn't ask a lot of questions."

"Oh Luke, I feel so guilty." She moaned. "It's all mixed up for me now. What do I do? What do we do? You can't live here alone, you're not 18. I'm in college two hours from here. I live in a dorm, at least until the end of the semester. There's some insurance, but we've lost his income and the house is not yet paid for. Neither of us makes enough to stay here. And do we really want to? There are so many memories. How do we decide?" She reached for the bottle and drained the last of the beer.

Luke took the empty bottle from her and set it behind them on the ground behind the log. He took her hands in his, warming them between his gloves. "Uncle Jack asked me to live with them," he said. "I turned him down."

Anna's eyes widened. "When did that happen?"

"The night dad died."

"Why didn't you tell me?" asked Anna.

"I don't know. I just know what I don't want, and it's not more abuse from Uncle Jack. He and dad are just the same. My friend Steve's family is willing to let me stay with them. Maybe I can live with you after we figure out what to do with the house, and you get settled somewhere with a little more space?"

"That means you'd have to change schools before you finish high school. After this semester I could come here and finish school online. Or I could just drop out for now. We don't yet know if we can't keep the house. It's a lot to think about."

"Yeah," he said. "It is. Let's go back to the house. At least it's warm there."

She reached for him and they hugged tightly for a long slow moment. Then he stood up and pulled her to her feet. They walked back to the house, leaving the empty bottle behind, sitting in the cold snow by the log.

***

Margaret Maurer is an aspiring writer, whose focus is poetry and short stories. She is enjoying the growth and development of this post-retirement career after a career as a Librarian and Cataloger at Kent State University Libraries, and at several Ohio Public Libraries. She lives in the lush and hilly northern woods of Ohio with her family and friends.

ONE MORE TIME

By Lana Wayne Koehler

He took off his gloves and laid them on the log beside her. Nuzzling his face into her jet-black hair that smelled like coconut, he whispered, "Don't worry. It will all be over soon."

"I don't believe you. It's NEVER over soon." She looked away from him and turned her gaze to the bottle she was holding. "This isn't my first rodeo."

Nathalie had been through in-patient therapy before. She knew the drill: take away everything she depended on. The last time, it almost killed her. Or at least she wanted to die. Maybe this time she would really die.

Victor held her closer. "This time will be different. This time you'll get the help you need. This time I'll be waiting for you at the end."

He was right. All of the other times she had no one waiting for her. There was no one to keep her sane. Nathalie knew that she had to make this work. The court would be checking up on her and monitoring her progress. If only...

"One last sip." She brought the bottle to her mouth and hesitated. Smelling the yeasty brew she took a deep breath to allow the aroma of the familiar to burn in her memory. Slowly the bottle touched her lips. The smoothness of the glass caressed them like a lover, and she took time with her tongue to roll the liquid around in her mouth. She would miss this as much as any relationship she had ever had. Even the one with Victor.

They had met at an Al-Anon meeting for children of abusive parents.

His father had abandoned his mother when he was very young. Even though he was only two when his father left, Victor swears that he remembers him.

"I know this sounds crazy, but I remember his laugh. It was a loud, boisterous sound that everyone knew was his trademark. I was out shopping at the mall once and something struck me as funny so I laughed out loud. I had a perfect stranger come up to me and say, 'Hey, aren't you

Fred's son?' That's when I knew for sure that I remembered him—and his laugh." Victor smiled with his eyes as well as his mouth. As the smile faded, he looked down, pretending to brush a piece of lint off of his jacket, but it was clear that he would break down if he went any farther in this talk about his father.

"I guess it was our similarities that drove my mother crazy. She would always say, 'You're just like your father', or 'You'll leave me just like he did.' Then she'd lapse into a drunken coma. At least she didn't hit me while she was passed out. She was right. I left as soon as I could. I couldn't wait to be out of there." Victor paused. "Fourteen is pretty young to be out on the streets, but it was better than living with her."

Nathalie came from what they told her was "family dysfunction". Nathalie's story was different. She came from a "loving family" with a father, mother, sister, and brother. What was her problem, anyway?

"My father expected me to be perfect—a perfect student, a perfect artist, a perfect daughter. Boy, was he wrong! I was so imperfect that it became a joke around the house. But it wasn't funny to me. The barbs and the insults flew like bullets in a war zone, and just as deadly.

"'Why didn't you nail that audition? You should have made that 'A'! Who do you think you are, talking back to me?' My father would criticize everything I did."

"That didn't stop him from trying to mold me into whatever he thought I could be for him. He used punishments to control me. The worst was that there were no boundaries in the family. My sister could take whatever she wanted of mine with no consequences. My brother could do whatever he wanted. I was the one made responsible for everyone's everything."

All along, my mother reminded him, and me, how really imperfect I was. She would glare at me with contempt and speak unspeakable things under her breath." Nathalie looked straight ahead but she could feel Victor's eyes penetrate her very being. Maybe he really understood her pain. "My mother's threats to disown me or hurt herself on my behalf would never stop."

"This was the yin and yang of my life, each pulling me into different directions expecting, or not expecting, me to deliver on their assessment of me. Until one day I broke. I went off the deep end of drinking to drown myself, literally. I broke so badly that it scared me. It scared me to think that I might not make it. It scared me to think that I would make it and have to start all over again." She looked over to see Victor's head bent down, as though he was praying. When he looked up, she saw the single tear trickling down his cheek. That was enough to solidify their relationship.

"So, here we are, two broken people." Victor carefully lifted his hand to move a strand of hair behind her ear.

"Some of us are more broken than others. Don't forget that, Victor." She moved away from him just an inch, but it might as well have been a mile. "You didn't drive drunk. You didn't run over that poor woman. You didn't almost kill her baby."

There it was, the chasm between them. Always a competition. Who was better? Who was worse?

"Listen, little girl, I've done lots of things in my past to survive. Things I'm not proud of, things I can't even tell you, but bad things nonetheless." Victor moved away this time. Was it shame? Was it protectiveness? "It doesn't matter now. We're on a path to recovery. Together. No longer alone. That's what I've always wanted. You. And me. Together. Forever."

He leaned over to kiss her. Nathalie flinched, but he was as persistent as he was gentle.

She suddenly flung her arms around him in an exaggerated motion that almost knocked them both onto to leaf-laden forest floor.

"Go ahead! Kiss me now! Kiss me like you mean it!" Nathalie didn't wait for him to answer. She grabbed him and drew him close, startling herself as much as him. "I love you, Victor. No matter what happens, know that I love you."

He kissed her in a way that he'd never kissed her before. He didn't want to let her go. "I love you, too." He brushed her hair back from her face. "I'll always love you."

Nathalie smiled, got up from the log, and brushed herself off. A piece of dry leaf stuck to her pant leg and no matter how hard she tried to swat it away, it wouldn't move. "Stubborn. Just like me." She took a long look at Victor. "I'm ready."

She turned away and ran as fast as she could, jumping over logs and brush, navigating the forest like a pro until she stopped in her tracks. She took one last look at Victor, who was bent over and out of breath from trying to keep up with her. He smiled at her as though he was enjoying the game.

"Goodbye, Victor." Nathalie smiled back and then turned to jump off of the cliff before her and into the abyss.

It was over soon, just as Victor had predicted.

***

Lana Wayne Koehler is a former music teacher. Her books include Ah-Choo! (Sterling) and Dine and Discuss Party Books (Third Thursday Publishing). She is a contributing member to various blogs, and has been a guest speaker at local universities, schools, writers groups, and the Society of Children's Book Writers and Illustrators.

ALL IT TAKES IS ONE

by Kelly C. Brown

Yesterday I was browsing Facebook, and I saw a picture stating that, "the average person walks past a murderer 36 times in their life." Surely, this is an extraordinary claim, and extraordinary claims require extraordinary evidence, which of course, the Facebook article didn't provide. But yet, does it really matter if it's 36 murderers? What if it's actually only 12 murderers; is that better for each of us? What if one of them is your barista at your coffee shop or the lady that bags your groceries for you? You get a coffee or your sack of produce and go on your way in ignorant bliss if you're not their target. And then again, sometimes just one murderer is enough, if you're the one they're looking for. On occasion, all it takes is one.

I sat on the cold stone wall in the park, drinking my third beer of the morning. My long brown hair fell over the shoulder of my pink parka and hid my face from him. When I spoke, my words came out in white puffs of frost. "Dr. Burke says its time, Peter." Tears slid down my icy cheeks. "He says it's for my own good, so that I can live a normal life."

"Whatever that bastard shrink thinks normal means." Peter sneered into my ear, as he hunched over me, his hands clenching my shoulders, wrinkled with cold, while his blue hoodie shielded his face. I could feel his pain through his anger. We had been together for so long, for most of my life. Peter had been my rock when I was just a pretty little three-year-old enduring unspeakable things from my father. He had comforted me as I cried in my bed after my mother had viciously slapped me across the face and called me a whore, when I finally gathered my courage to tell her what my father, her husband, had been doing to me for years. Peter was the older, stronger, brother figure that had kept me living, and helped me survive my childhood. And now Dr. Burke thought Peter's influence over me, his sheer presence in my life, was so disruptive that Peter had to leave me alone...forever.

The choice was an agonizing one that no person should ever have to make. Banish your brother, your friend, your literal life-saver for a chance to live a normal life, to put the hideous past and its' damage to your psyche behind you. How could I make the decision? Me? The stupid little three-year old who had believed her daddy had loved her because he raped her; who believed her mother's curses that she was evil and deserved what she got for tempting her father. I had never stood up for myself, not once, the way Peter had stood up for me. It had been Peter who had once and for all put a stop to my father's abuse when I had slit my wrists prepared to die at age eleven. When they found my father, in that alleyway beside his auto mechanic shop, with his throat slit from ear to ear, the police looked for a rival business man, a gang member. They never looked in our own home, at the mousy wife, or the depressed child. And a few years later when my mother had fallen down our home's steep concrete steps into the basement and broken her neck, the social services worker just shook her head over me, the poor parent-less teenager, now sentenced to the foster care system. But I knew Peter had protected me again, liberated me, because his love for me was that strong.

"Don't do it, Em" Peter was hissing into my ear now. I downed my beer and reached for a fourth. I was due at Dr. Burke's office in 15 minutes, at 9:00 a.m. bright and early. Dr. Burke had prepared me for this moment, in the previous 15 months of sessions I had had with him. At first, our sessions had been court-ordered by my social services case manager, and I had been forced to attend, resentful and uncooperative, with Peter tagging along to watch over me. But I had begun to reluctantly like and then trust Dr. Burke, and at his suggestion had told Peter he wasn't allowed to come with me any longer. There were things that Dr. Burke and I had to talk about, to plan for my future, my return to living like a "normal" person, and I knew Peter wouldn't understand why I wanted it.

How do you explain to the one person who kept you alive and going through the worst years of your life, who took the razor out of your hand and bound your wrists, and then killed your tormentors for you? How do you tell that person who loved you more than you loved yourself, that for you to become healthy with any chance at a happy life, it's time for them to go, to disappear from your life? For if they stay, you will never be free of your past, always reminded, always condemned to be held in its grasp.

I jumped up, shaking free of Peter's hands still roughly grasping my shoulders. "Enough Peter," I violently threw my beer bottle against the low stone wall, shattering it into pieces. "I've made my mind up. It's time I save my own life for once."

An hour later I sat in Dr. Burke's office staring down at his body lying next to his desk, his head a pulpy mess. Peter was calmly replacing a small stone Buddha statue covered in the doctor's blood back on top of his desk. Wiping his hands on his jeans, Peter smiled broadly at me. "That was a close call, Em. That bastard almost had you talked into killing me off."

I shook my head from side to side. What had gone on in here? "Oh my God, Peter, what have you done?" I wailed. "Dr. Burke was a good man. He was just trying to help me, he just wanted me to …"

"Yeah, yeah, reintegration of an alternate identity, I read your file, Em." Peter's voice took on an eerily high-pitched tone, "Emily Peterson, Dissociative identity disorder, formerly known as multiple personality disorder, resulting from extensive childhood sexual abuse, one alter, older male, Peter, protector, suspected of killing at least one family member." Peter shook the case file which had been lying on the desk at Em, blood spatters hitting her face. 'Get real, Em, he wanted you to kill me off. Me. I protected you all those years. Got anyone who hurt you out of your way. And this is how you repay me, by plotting to kill me? No one kills me off, Em. You got that? You, or anyone else who tries to, is in for a surprise."

You can only walk by a murderer on the street if they got away with the murder, did you realize that? The average person probably only kills one person while TV tells us everyone is a serial killer. I wonder which of those is the truth.

How many people do you walk by in a day? I bet if you live in a big city you might feel anonymous, safer. But I live in a big city; maybe we've walked by each other today? These are the things I think about as Peter and I walk away from Dr. Burke's office.

I think most often the motive for murder is shockingly personal. So, ask yourself, what have you done to anger a murderer?

But I digress, since what does any of this matter when the murderer is you?

***

Kelly C. Brown, J.D., CHt. is a Master Clinical Hypnotherapist in private practice, and a Professor of Complementary and Alternative Medicine at Walsh University, North Canton, Ohio. She teaches Meditation classes at several women's wellness centers for trauma survivors and advocates. Kelly is a retired psychiatric disability law attorney and worked for twenty years with veterans and civilians with PTSD. She is a co-author of *Seven Deadly Sins: Simply Delectable Stories*, with Third Thursday Publishing, LLC.

MAYBE YOU AREN'T REALLY LOOKING FOR NEW IDEAS...

Perhaps you don't have writer's block and you aren't looking for story ideas. But there are other ways that photos can be inspirational and instrumental in moving your writing along.

Maybe you have plot ideas, but are looking for the ideal setting. Perusing photos of natural outdoor settings, house, hut, or castle interiors, or illustrations of fantasy and sci-fi worlds might lead to just the right spot for the world you want for your particular book. You may even find a more intriguing spot than the one you originally thought you wanted. A photo can form the basis for the world-building you need to do to make it feel real to your readers.

While you might have ideas for your characters, looking at photos of people can sometimes help you define your characters more specifically. You might even run across better characters for your story, characters you never thought of but now want to include, or characters that might serve to take your story in a totally different direction from where you first started.

Writing a photo plots story could just serve to give you a break from the novel you are currently writing and, if you are stuck on a chapter, or the plot just isn't working, writing something unrelated can often get your mind renewed and ready to return to your novel.

Never underestimate the power of visual suggestion on a writer's brain. You may be amazed at where the inspiration of photographs might take you.

CHAPTER FIVE: THE PHOTOS: SETTINGS

As you look through the pictures and decide what stories you want to tell, remember that the questions about setting and world-building will not all apply to every picture. Use all the sensory details, sights, smells, tastes, sounds, touch, to make your reader feel like he or she is right there with you.

Photo Plots

Photo Plots

Science Fiction and Fantasy

This section consists of illustrations, not photographs, in order to provide setting ideas for writers who love to write science fiction and fantasy. Keep in mind the world-building considerations: consistency, religions, mythology, ethics, politics, communication, technology, transportation, weather, language, clothing, money, and human connections to fantasy creatures, if any.

Photo Plots

CHAPTER SIX: THE PHOTOS: CHARACTERS

Review the questions to ask about who your characters are, their likes and dislikes, their fears, their passions and motivations. Think about what might have brought them to this point in the picture; it may serve as the catalyst that will give you the ideas for your story.

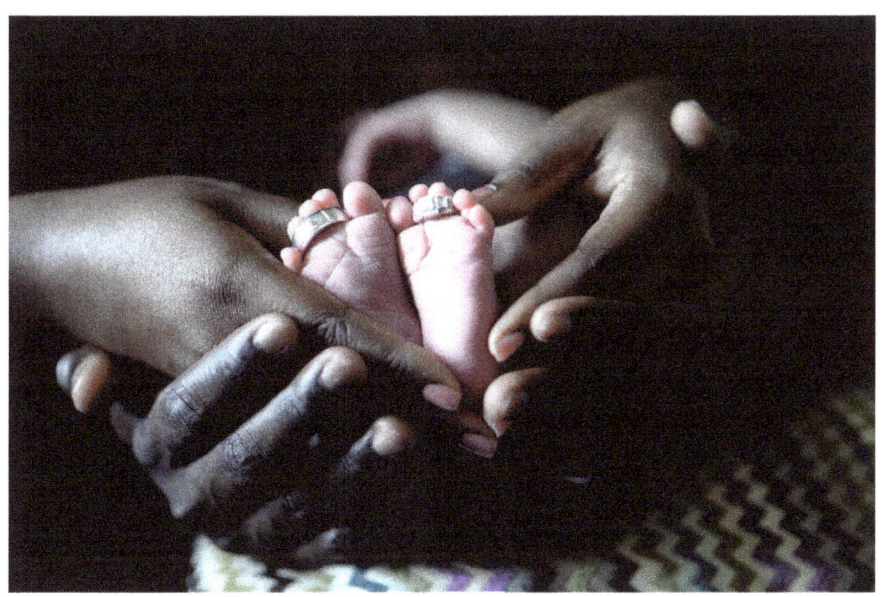

Photo Plots

Animals

Include lots of sensory details in your stories about animals.
Will you turn them into talking animals for a fantasy novel?
Will they be realistic stories about animal abuse and protection?
How will they relate to the people in your story?
Where will these pictures take you?

Photo Plots

CHAPTER SEVEN: RESOURCES FOR WRITERS

The writing community can be a very generous group. We are held together by the common knowledge that this can be a daunting and often frustrating business. Sharing resources and experiences is one way to help and support one another. I hope that some of these resources will be of help to you.*

Books:

Bird by Bird by Anne LaMott, Anchor, 1995.

Bootcamp for Novelists BEYOND THE FIRST DRAFT: Writing Techniques of the Pros by Linda Style, LMS Press, 2013.

Hooked: Write Fiction That Grabs Readers at Page One & Never Lets Them Go by Les Edgerton, Writer's Digest Books, 2007.

How I Write: Secrets of a Bestselling Author by Janet Evanovich and Ina Yalof, St. Martin's Griffin, 2006.

How to Make a Living as a Writer by James Scott Bell, Compendium Press, 2014.

How to Make a Living with Your Writing: Books, Blogging and More by Joanna Penn, Curl Up Press, 2015.

How to Write a Romance Novel: Getting it Written and Getting it Published by Susan Palmquist, Create Space, 2016.

Liz Fielding's Little Book of Writing Romance: How to Write Bestselling Romantic Fiction by Liz Fielding. Classic Romance Publishing, 2012.

Write Worlds Your Readers Won't Forget by Stant Litore, Westmarch Publishing, 2017.

Write Your Novel From the Middle: A New Approach for Plotters, Pantsers, and Everyone In Between by James Scott Bell, Compendium Press, 2014.

Writer's Market by Robert Lee Brewer, Writer's Digest, 2019.

Writing Dynamite Story Hooks: A Masterclass in Genre Fiction and Memoir by Jackson Dean Chase, Jackson Dean Chase, Inc., 2018.

Writing Irresistible Kidlit: The Ultimate Guide to Crafting Fiction for Young Adult and Middle Grade Readers by Mary Kole, Writer's Digest, 2012.

Writing the Breakout Novel: Insider Advice for Taking Your Fiction to the Next Level by Donald Maas, Writer's Digest, 2002.

You Can Write a Mystery by Gillian Roberts, Untreed Reads, 2014.

Your Personal Fiction-Writing Coach: 365 Days of Motivation & Tips to Write a Great Book! by Stephanie Bond, Need to Read Books, 2015.

Your Writing Coach by Jurgen Wolff, Nicholas Breely, 2007.

Websites:

Ann Kroeker, writing coach: http://annkroeker.com/

Editing service: www.two4onekidcritiques.com

Fiction Notes: www.darcypattison.com

Fiction University: http://blog.janicehardy.com/

Freelance Writing: https://www.freelancewrit

Funds for Writers: www.fundforwriters.com

Helping Writers Become Authors:

https://www.helpingwritersbecomeauthors.com/#

Jane Friedman: www.janefriedman.com

Joanna Penn: www.thecreativepenn.com

Live, Write, Thrive: https://www.livewritethrive.com/

Plot Generator: https://www.plot-generator.org.uk/

The Purple Crayon: www.underdown.org

Well Storied: https://www.well-storied.com/

Writerology: https://www.writerology.net/

Writers Helping Writers: https://writershelpingwriters.net/

*While these sources are currently available at printing, please note that websites and books are often discontinued and some of these may not be available at a future date.

A Note from the Author

Although I wrote this book to give writers a concrete format and specific questions to help them create strong stories from the photos and illustrations in this book, I also realize that part of the magic of writing is that our brains are able to contrive such unique and wonderful ideas during the writing process that they needn't always be constrained by traditional formats and templates. So please, feel free to take any inspiration you may derive from the photos in this book and write the stories in the way that works best for you.

Gloria G. Adams is a freelance writer and former librarian from Ohio. She has been published by Sterling Children's Books, Schoolwide, Inc., Rosen, Greenhaven Press, Enslow, Third Thursday Publishing, and the Children's Writer's and Illustrator's Market. She is a member of the Society of Children's Book Writers and Illustrators (SCBWI) and the Alliance of Independent Authors (ALLi.) She and co-founder, author Jean Daigneau, run a critique editing service, Two-4-One Kid Critiques, LLC: www.two4onekidcritiques.com.

For more information, visit her websites, http://gloriagadams.com and http://slantedink.com.

Gloria G. Adams

www.ingramcontent.com/pod-product-compliance
Lightning Source LLC
Chambersburg PA
CBHW061224070526
44584CB00029B/3974